MW01671238

The Free Range Poets Society

Drabifordian Academy Poetry Project 2015

Funding to print the collection was provided by

CWP Fairfield
Connecticut Writing Project

Fairfield
UNIVERSITY

The Free Range Poets Society

Drabifordian Academy Poetry Project 2015

The Connecticut Writing Project Fairfield University

 ISBN: 9780990462965

Publisher:	The Connecticut Writing Project, Fairfield University
Editor:	Carol Ann Davis
Contributing Editors:	Dione Sordi and Kristina Tartaglia

Acknowledgments:
Gratitude is expressed Maura Drabik and Todd Stentiford, who together foster such an open and inviting atmosphere and community in the classroom all year that poetry naturally flourishes. Thank you also to Anne Uberti and Jill Beaudry for welcoming the program to Reed, and Dione Sordi and Kristina Tartaglia for assisting with the poetry lessons and compilation process.

At Fairfield University, thanks to support provided by: Chair Elizabeth Petrino and the Department of English; Professor Bryan Ripley Crandall and The Connecticut Writing Project; Melissa Quan and the Office of Service Learning; Professor Elizabeth Boquet and The Writing Center; Interim Dean James Simon and The Humanities Institute, College of Arts and Sciences. The collection was printed in collaboration with the Poetry in Communities Project at Fairfield University.

Contents

The Free Range Poets Society: An Introduction

The first thing you notice when you enter the two-class cluster led by Maura Drabik and Todd Stentiford is the freedom of movement. Students are free to move about the classroom, finding the spot where they feel they can best learn, think, and create. It's no wonder, then, that poetry enters such a space easily, and that miracles ensue. Given free range, these poets—Drabifordians, as they call themselves—wander and dip, meander and theorize, leap about and sometimes even fly.

The poems included in this collection are the culmination of a six-lesson poetry unit undertaken by the cluster in May of 2015. In the first three lessons, students explored the world of the five senses (Sensory Riddle Poems), joked and teased about moments in which they were both sorry and not (False Apology poems), and described themselves—and eventually their whole class (see page 58)—in terms of metaphor (Metaphor Portraits). The final three lessons invited humor into the poems when students invented cliché mash-ups (Ten Minute Spills), encouraged self-reflection and self-valuing in poems of praise (Praise Poems) and finally embarked upon collaborative rather than individual composition in the final day of Around the Table poems. An index of poets is provided at the end of the collection for easy reference.

As educators, it's amazing to have gotten to hear and learn from each of you. As moms, there is nothing better than seeing your child happy, among friends, and expressing him or herself freely. Free Range Poets, every day that we got to spend hearing you read from your work, or laugh and smile at the work of others, is a treasure we get to keep, even as you ready yourselves to leave Drabifordian Academy well equipped to discover new experiences. Each of you leaves the comfort of this place having been a part of something very special all year. Enjoy returning to the magical place that was your sixth grade classroom every time you open these pages. And through these words may your parents and loved ones overhear a bit of the joy that will always be this cluster of which you were an indispensible part.

Warmly,

Carol Ann Davis (Willem Doherty's mom)
Dione Sordi (Luke Sordi's mom)
Kristina Tartaglia (Joseph Tartaglia's mom)

Sensory Riddle Poems

Poets wrote poems that engage with the five senses to describe objects or places; sometimes they named the poem's subject and sometimes they left it a riddle.

Untitled
By Douglas McIntyre

I follow you around as the sun is shines in the sky as it raises higher and higher you see me less and less as it goes down I go to sleep but when it raises I'm at your feet

Untitled
By Rushil Jerfy

I tower over all
A strong and sturdy body
Rough
Full of life
Swaying with the wind
Green as the grass until autumn arrives.

Untitled
By Rushil Jerfy

Claws like knives
A voice like a trumpet
Cunning and cruel
A fiery red mane
I am the king
Who am I?

Me

By Anne Marie Carlson

My name is Todd
And sometimes I find
The kids a little bit odd
I am a little stressed so I am
Going to go to listen to my
IPod
I help kids know they
Are right with a nod

The Chocolate Thunder

Joseph Bonsignore

Ah, the Chocolate Thunder from Outback. Truly a divine delicacy. The big warm brownie, the big scoop of ice cream on top, and the big scoop of whipped cream on top of that. You can remember that faint thud when the waiter/waitress sets it down on the table. They always bring multiple spoons, but I never share. You can smell the fresh, warm brownie from a mile away. When you are done gazing at its magnificence and take a bite, you feel the warm brownie and the cool ice cream combining in your mouth. The way the two flavors complement each other is what really makes it taste so good. And of course, the whipped cream is soft and creamy, and makes for an excellent topping. You don't need to worry about making the most out of it, because you'll definitely be coming back for another one.

I Will Come Back Next Year
By Julia Dolan

I am beautiful, and young for my age too.
Everyone exclaims over my looks, and ask where they can get one.
Insects glance at my beauty, and take a sip of my nectar.
I feel the gazes of my friends and admirers.
I am getting old, my petals beginning to wilt.
They will fall off soon.
I say good-bye to my friend Rose.
She says "Good-bye, Calla,"
I feel my heart start to break.
I will be back next year.
She will not.

Treasure
By Chelsea Fowler

As I lay on the cool, hard shelf
Squashed between my two friends
I wonder whose warm hands
I will be held in today

Between my pages I hold a treasure
An adventure, a mystery
Who knows what they will stumble upon
when they pick me up

I know the lucky person that holds me
will be met with a surprise

Stronger
By Julia Dolan

It is cold, and glorious outside.
I am surrounded by a beautiful, untouched, white blanket.
I pray that no one will step on me.
I know what happened to my mother.
Someone stepped on her, and she cracked.
I will not.
I will be strong, stronger than her.
I will live, and when spring comes, I will die in peace.

The Candle
By Jennifer Lorenz

When the sun goes away
And the moon comes to stay
I ignite
Pouring dim light
Into a room that appears night
The smell of smoke drips from my flame
Slowly fading away
As people are laughing, talking
Eating food while walking
As I pour dim light
Into the room that appears night
As people start to leave
I grieve
When I realize that my wax is melting
Until there is nothing
Now I cannot ignite
Cannot pour dim light
Not into that room that always appears night

Baseball Game!
By Trevor Jacozzi

The smell of popcorn is in the air
Hotdogs and peanuts are everywhere
At the crack of the bat the fans all cheer
Yelling and screaming in my ear
The crowd goes quiet when the ball hits the mitt
But I won't fear because my team won't quit!
I am a Yankees fan pride and true
I like to watch their games just like you
A-rod, Teixeira, and C.C too
Dominate the field wearing pinstripes that are white and blue
They make it look easy, make it look fun
They round the bases and run, run, run!

Trees
By Nicholas Fischer

I start off small
Then grow big.
I bloom in the spring
And look old in the fall
I am different shapes and sizes
I am never the same
Some people destroy me
And others keep me
I help out in the world

Pencil

By Nicholas Fischer

I am yellow
I could be different shapes
I mostly am #2
I help you do your homework
I help you do test
I help you learn
I help you write
I can break easily
But I can always come back

Clear

By Joanie Gogliettino

People see right through me, but they know I'm here.
I help those who have a hard time with seeing the good in others.
What's on the outside doesn't matter, it's what's on the inside.
People say that the soul is shone through the eyes,
and I'm a firm believer in that.
Clearer versions appear clearly in front of you like an open door.
So you are not deceived by anything.
No more blurry lines, just your straight path of justice.

Guitar

By Anna Mattioli

Wooden bridge
Long neck
Perfect tunes
Strummin blues
Sweet sounds of harmony
Hummin in the darkness
Singing in the light
Bigger than a banjo
Smaller than a bike
And now I'll be the only one
to play upon it
day and night.

Something

By Annie Fowler

Look under you there is something
Something that can come in all different colors
Something that can hold all your weight
Something that may squeak
Something that might smell very, very bad
Something that acts like tires for your body
Something that separates you from the earth
What is that something?

Dancing to the End (the Pen)

By Sophia Child

You used my brothers and sisters
And spilled their blood,
Black blood,
onto white
You force them
to dance
Until there is
no more blood left
When we are clustered together
in a blue pile
I hope that you
do not choose me
Now, you pick
me up into
your hot and wet
fingers
You thrust me
this way and that
Until
I am no longer

I am

By Annie Fowler

I am above you
I am used to see
I am bright
I am ?

What am I?
By Paige Farley

I am straight and pointy
Firm and dainty

You use me to sew
and to make bows

I am silver and exact
and I do not act

I am the thin line that
runs through the thread

I can be a machine
or I can be manual

I am the maker of most of your clothes
Who am I?

Porcupine
By Michael Patrick Elston

Prickly spiky not a hedge hog
don't scare me you'll regret it
and you especially won't forget it
my sharp armor protects me
I curl into a ball so
don't touch me

Idea

By Julian Totir

I am abandoned
Lost in a sea of thoughts
All yours
You made me
Breathed life into me
But you have disregarded me

You thought I was worthy
But you had a better one
That thought destroyed me

Imagine

By Juliana Miraldi

I can be twisted, morphed, shaped.
I can be squeezed, taunted, poked.
I can be squishy, or I can be hard.
I can be shown in many ways.
I can be used for hours on end.
I sound like a laughing child, look pastel like a rainbow.
I taste sweet like candy, until I am misused, and then I am bitter, like the darkness in the sky.

Time

By Juliana Miraldi

I am fragmented.
I am a heart of life.
I am a mind of time.
I tick by, I tick by.
I am green, I am color deep.
I am a young child strayed.
I am old man who is here to stay.
I tick by, I tick by.
I walk alone, I walk with all.
I talk to walls, and they talk back
I am a clock who's lost his time.
I tick by, I tick by.
I know the world, but world doesn't know me.
I am all, I am one.
I am a memory long forgot.
I tick by, I tick by.

The Universe

By Clayton Kunzweiler

Larger than life I'm always here.
You may hear the big bangs that happen inside of me.
You see me in the night with stars filling my space.
You are at a distance where there is no sense of touch, smell or taste.
Larger than life I'm always here, watching over you like the night sky.

Night

By Lauren Nalajala

Night falls, children leave, people go inside
Night falls, light fades away, the dark comes out to play
Night falls, animals prowl, every place becoming theirs
Night falls, doors are locked, and people hide the key
Night fades, the danger passes, like nothing was ever there

Untitled

By Lauren Nalajala

Untitled , unnamed, unwritten
Stories waiting to unfold
Untitled, unnamed, unwritten
Stories that are never told
Untitled, unnamed, unwritten
Into the traps that we are lured
Untitled, unnamed, unwritten
Always waiting to be heard

False Apology

Poets used William Carlos Williams's "This Is Just to Say" to write their own unapologetic apologies. Some poets drew from invented characters, historical figures, or figures from fairy tales.

Sorry Not Sorry
By Abby Poseno

This is just to say,
I broke your Ps4
controller.

In which you
Probably wanted
to use.

Forgive me,
you could use a
Break from video
games.

This Is Just To Say
By Collin Hoffman

I have forgotten
to put
the laundry
into the dryer

And which
you were going
to use
in the morning

Forgive me
I was playing
a game that was
so fun and exciting

Untitled
By Kaia Gioffre

I'm sorry for dropping my violin.
Im sorry for making you go and get it fixed.
I'm sorry for getting a lower grades because of my dropping
my violin.
I'm sorry but at least I don't have to practice anymore.

Untitled
By Susannah Drap

Dear Andrew, I have
hit you with a baseball on
your 11th birthday

You probably wanted
to enjoy your 11th birthday

Forgive me for hitting you
with a baseball when you
were annoying me

I'm sorry poem
By Trevor Jacozzi

I'm sorry
That I made
You sad by bulling
You, I know I broke your
Heart if you love me you will
Forgive me and we can have a fresh start

Match Over

By Jennifer Lorenz

Ooh Sorry
I may have just won the game
Possibly the set
And match
By putting spin on the ball
And slamming it in your face
So you didn't even have time to swing your racket
You might have a black eye too
Maybe
But I have to admit
The look on your face was priceless
And the trophy is smooth and shiny

Sorry not sorry poem

By Paige Psichopaidas

I may have tried to pick you up chipmunk.

And which you probably didn't exactly enjoy.

Forgive me you were so cute and fluffy you stole my
heart until you almost attacked me.

Untitled
By Jenna Reilly

I have taken that $20 you left (so conveniently I must add)
in plain sight on the kitchen counter

you were probably saving it for a video game, although now
I may never know if that is the case.

I used it very wisely on an itunes gift card and a chocolate bar
forgive me once more...
Yours truly

Sorry, Not Sorry
By Allie Luby

I have thrown all
your stuff out the window,
You shouldnt have left it
in plain sight.

I know you
might need it,
but it was very fun.

Forgive me,
it was too
delightful. So fun,
so exhilarating

Scratch

By C.J. Demers

Sorry I scratched your car
but I hit the ball really far

I know you wanted to relax
since you just buffed and waxed

At least I'm getting better and I didn't
scratch your favorite sweater

I know I scratched your car
and if I do it again I'll run real far

Sorry Not Sorry

By Jack Street

This Is Just To Say...

I have eaten
the last cookie
that was in the jar

you were probably
going to have it for a snack
but I ate it for dessert

whoops
it smelled so good
and it tasted even better

This is Just to say...
By Hannah Sepp

It was an accident I bruised your your forehead with acorn,
I was my natural reflexes
That fateful day in my backyard,

I know
you just wanted to say hello
I did not at all giggle,
well maybe a little
but the acorn imprint on you head was pretty amusing

From me to you I am sorry
I feared for your life
you looked kind of dazed
But you were a little imposing
Plus there were acorns
all
around
me!

Dust
By Clayton Kunzweiler

I just left you in the dust,
it was only in front of the parents.

You tried to stay with me,
but I was too good.

I apologize, it felt so good,
the look on your face was priceless.

Cookies

By Shaine Luzietti

I ate the cookies
you were saving
for dessert
last night.

I thought you were
saving them
for me.

I'm sorry,
but
they were so
delicious.

Wrestling

By Shaine Luzietti

I beat you
in a wrestling match,
where I used
my best move.

I know
you were hoping
to win.

But this trophy
fits perfectly with
my collection.

False Apology
By Zack Majeski

I'm sorry for the apples,
Sorry for the bread,
Sorry that I threw them at Ryan Carson's head,
Sorry that I ripped apart Jason Smith's robot,
But most of all I'm sorry that I got caught.

Untitled
By Patrick Sonne

I have stolen
the strawberry pop
and jumped on the neighbors
trampoline

you were going to
use them for
Pizza night
too bad

I apologize
my favorite flavor
sweet and fizzy
so good

This Is Just To Say
By Michael Haddick

I have rang
your doorbell
and then
bolted away

Expecting someone
visiting you
opened the door
but not a thing

Forgive me
I enjoyed the grace
of the confused
look upon your face

Cat and Mouse
By Willem Doherty

This is just to say
I have run
Right under your feet
And made you trip
And you were probably using those feet
To walk down the stairs
Forgive me
But–
Whoa!
Watch out!
There is a string

This is just to say

By Brynn Reilly

I have opened
the cookies
box that was
in the pantry

and which
you were probably
saving
for dessert

Forgive me
they were delicious
so chewy
and so sweet

Untitled

By Julian Totir

Good morning
I have just
Woken you up from
A good night's sleep

Even though you were
Wanting to
Sleep in
This morning

Forgive me
Even though you are
Probably still half asleep
I am hungry

Metaphor Portraits

Poets wrote poems that described themselves in metaphorical terms.

Have Heart
By Elijah Baraw

Do not worry,
For I am the shadow galloping with you,
The Sun rising above your head.
For I am the Dreams you pursue,
The fire burning, raging inside you.
For I am the Hope coursing through your veins,
The passion smoldering in your heart.
I am the Moon, looking upon the fear
resting on your shoulders.
You see me in everything you look to,
For I am all the Light you cannot see.

Comment: Never give up, for your loved ones are always with you.

Small And Big
By Abby Poseno

I am one grain of sand on a beach,
I am one star in the night sky,
I am one wave in the ocean,
I am one fish in the sea,
I am one rose in a field of sunflowers,
I am one snowflake, special in my own way,
I am one page in a book,
I am one cloud in the sky,
I am one raindrop in a storm,
I am one person in the world.

I am

By Anne Marie Carlson

I am a bright pink spring flower
I am a cup of coffee on a cold winter morning
I am a church bell ringing at noon
I an angel coming down from heaven (says my mom
I am a dandelion losing its last petal
I am a work in progress
I believe in all natures and I believe in all cultures
I believe in many diverse frames of mind
I am the frozen heart of winter
I am a graceful swan floating along the watery streams
I am a piece of sugary candy waiting to be bought in a store
I am the waves rippling in the ocean
I am a cat trying to get milk
I am a piece of cut wire
I am a camera capturing every moment of every day
I am a piece of gum
As a community we are a leprechaun trying to get to the other side of the rainbow

I am

By Chelsea Fowler

I am the sweet sound of crickets
Once the darkness has come
I am the white rose
In the garden of red
I am the wild one
Running the other way
I am the beauty
In a sea of ugly
I am one

Poem of Collin

By Collin Hoffman

I am a rabbit gnawing on a carrot
I am a fish rolling in the sea
I am a deer running through the woods
I am a plant growing in the sunlight
I am a wolf dashing after my prey
I am a bird gliding through the air
I am a groundhog eating grass
I am a turtle swimming in the ocean
I am a seal lying in the sun
I am a shooting star in the midnight sky.
But most of all I am Collin.

Untitled

By Noelle Salley

i am a deer in the headlights
i am the dark clouds on a sunny day
i am a star far, far away
i am the sound of rain
i am the snow melting away in the spring
i am a mouse creeping past a cat
i am wild like a tiger
i am a snowflake, disappearing when seen
i am the moon, only parts of me show
you see, i am different

I Am

By Chase Yeaton

I am many things.
I am the jungle's tiger,
brave and bold.
I am the sky's eagle,
a bird's eye view.
I am the tree's fruit,
sweet and sour.
I am many things.
I am the sun's light,
happy and true.
I am the moon's light,
shiny and new.
I am my own cloud,
going anywhere.
I am am many things.
I am me.

Metaphor Poem

By Emilee Christopher

I am a blade of grass in a meadow
I am a fresh drop of dew in the morning grass
I am a creek in the misty forest
I am a leaf gliding down from a oak tree
I am a lily pad in a pond
I am a horse galloping in the meadow
I am a ocean wave crashing against the sand
I am a sneaker running on a track
I am a breeze on a summer evening
I am the black keys on the grand piano

Untitled

By Jenna Reilly

I am like a flower blossoming every year.
I am like a toaster heating up (getting mad)
but cooling down within a few minutes
I am like a lightbulb, my ideas as my power
I am like a turtle going very slowly, but
finally reaching my goals
I am like a cheetah, life moving by
in the blink of an eye
I am like a grain of sand surrounded
by others
I am a work in progress
I am one person as of 7 billion
I am Jenna Reilly!

I am poem

By Paige Psichopaidas

I am the shooting star that flies through the sky
I am the sweet apple in the picnic baskets
I am shining when everything is dark
I am the rainbow after a tornado
I am the light at the end of a tunnel
I am the only book on the shelves
I am the only rose in the garden
I am sweet when everyone is sour
I am kind when everyone is mean
I am the only dog in the park
I am me

ME

By C.J. Demers

I am a hawk soaring in the sky
I am a fish swimming in the ocean
I am a tree taller than all
I am an ant as small as can be
I am a lion roaming free
I am the sun that lightens every ones day
I am the stars that give you hope at night
I am me

Me

By Joseph Bonsignore

I am the green potato chip in the bag
I am the shiny pokemon you spent hours trying to get (it's a
  one in 4,000 something chance, 8,000 something
  chance if you're playing one of the older games.)
I am an array of bright colors
I am a tower of blocks that could fall over at the slightest touch
I am a wheel of fortune, unpredictable and changing
I am surrounded by spikes
I am that one winning lottery ticket
I am that expensive defective amiibo (they're little action figures)
I am that person that stands out from the crowd
I am unique. I am creative. I am me.

We are legos, interlocking to create the perfect creation

Who I Am
By Sophia Child

I am the falcon's dive

I am the eagle's swoop

I am the owl's call

I am the hawk's flight

I am strong

I am brave

I can fly, I can fly

I am the dove's peace

I am the robin's egg

I am the swan's feather

I am the bluejay's song

I am unique

I am one and only

I can fly, I can fly

I am Poem

By Kate Farrington

I am a cloud in the sky
I am the sun in the rainbow
I am the shooting star at night
I am the leaf in the air
I am a blooming peddle of the flowe
I am the unique dog in the park
I am a rainbow after the thunderstorm
I am the only footprint in central park
I am the pot of gold at the end of the rainbow
I am the sunflower in an all rose garden
I am the only bow tie in the store
I am the only book on the book shelf
I ma the only soccer ball on the field
I am the one mixed in the crowd
I am the only one wearing a bright shirt at a wedding
I am the bright cloud in the dark sky
I am unique

Metaphor Poem

By Zack Majeski

I am the mystery of the universe.
I am a dog drooling on wood floors.
I am ice, yes, slippery, painful ice.
I am the last dodo bird.
I am a narwhal swimming in the ocean.
I am the fourth person in a third-person narrative.
I am a stone left unturned.
I am the forgotten forget-me-not.
I am me.

Me

By Joanie Gogliettino

My hair is the grass, swaying in the wind weightless.
My heart is a rock, heavy with many possessions.
My arms are birds, playing with the wind happily.
My brain is a vine, twisting and clinging to every moment it can hold onto.
My legs are leopards, elegant and agile.
My heart is a drum, pounding only with kindness and compassion.
My knees are trees, standing strong, but are threatened to be cut down.
My feet are a tune being strummed delicately.
I am many things, but most of all, I am Joanie.

I Am Me

By Allie Luby

I am a number on the endless number line
I am a student in a class
I am a leaf on a tree
I am a fish behind a glass
I am who I am and,
I am one of many

I am the one and only
I am the scholar, to me
I am a red leaf next to a million green
I am Free to live my life
I am who I am and,
I am one of a kind there is none like me

I am
By Bridget Gogliettino

I am a star shining bright
I am the world full of life
I am the peacemaker
I am the tree hugger
I am the one that cares for the world
I stay timid and shy
I hide my face
But now I learn showing my true colors isn't such
  a bad thing anymore

Untitled
By Patrick Sonne

I am many things
I am as hard as a stone
But as soft as a pillow
As large as the largest mountain
but as dinky as a atom
I am as valuable as a diamond
But as worthless as a pebble
I am the rain
I am the lion
I am a blanket
I am the light
I am hot I am cold
I am peace
I am war
But in the end I am one thing
I am me

Stand Out

By Jack Street

I am a snowflake in a snowstorm
I am a raindrop in a rainstorm
I am a cloud in a blue sky
I am a bright star in the dark sky
I am a blade of grass in a lawn
I am a leaf on a tree
I am a spot on a cheetah
I am a stripe on a zebra
But most of all,
I am not the same as anyone else

I am a Loop

By Luke Sordi

I am myself,
Changing with my surroundings.
I am my surrounding,
Changing colors.
I am a color,
Changing with my emotions.
I am an emotion,
Changing with the people around me.
I am the people around me,
Changing ideas like clothes.
I am my clothes,
Changing to express my thoughts.
I am my thoughts,
Changing where I am.
I am where I am,
Changing

Bright or Dark?

By Paige Farley

I am a bush up in the dark night forest

I am a star up in the dark milky way sky

I am a piano key that goes up and down

I am a big, fluffy cloud in the daylight

I am a giving tree in the open woods

I am a rainbow that flows through the bright skies

I am a dark, gray cloud up in the stormy sky

I am the bright, orange ball that bounces down the court

I am the bright, bold moon up in the dark and dreamy night sky

I have my ups and I have my downs

So does that make me bright or does that make me dark?

Sports
By John Sullivan

I am a black and white soccer ball rolling in the morning grass

I am a small yellow tennis ball being tossed back n forth

I am a hard lax ball being thrown with a twist of the wrist

I am a hard orange ball going swish

I am a brown oval pigskin scoring points

I am a white volleyball in the sand

I am a hard ball that sits on a tee

I am the puck that slides on the ice

I am the ball with stitching that hits a homeroom

I never stop moving

I am
By Brynn Reilly

I am the light at the end of a tunnel
I am a rose in a garden of sunflowers
I am optimistic when everyone is sad
I am giving when everyone is selfish
I am the rainbow in a thunder storm
I am loud when everyone is quiet
I am light when everything is dark
I am kind when everyone is mean
I am the color in a newspaper
I am the moon in a sky of stars
I am unique

Won't
By Willem Doherty

I am the wail of a whale
I am Socrates' grandfather clock
I am the Enigma code
I am Leopold Bloom
I am the glint of rust
I am first person to third person shift
Take that, Conciseness!
I am the pop of sheets
I am special
I am made up of only tiny little things
My atoms have been here since the beginning of time
I am made up of only tiny little things
They will be here after I am gone
I am made up of only tiny little things
They won't remember me

I am...
By Anna Romano

I am light, sometimes dark
I am stone cold
I am a firework at night
I am a snowflake in a snowstorm
I am ice
I am fire
I am sometimes a liar
I am human
And so are you

Ten Minute Spills

Using an exercise adapted from *The Practice of Poetry* (Ed. Robin Behn), poets utilized a word bank (with words such as blueberries, cloud, lick, mother) to transform clichés (such as "don't count your chickens before they hatch") into humorous ten-line poems, in the space of ten minutes.

Untitled

By Adem Selmani

cat got your mom
i left my blackberry on
mother is sleeping
your cat is licking your curtains
you rolled of the cliff

Changing up Some Phrases

By Ashley Reed

Jumping off the bandwagon
Jumping off the cliff
Don't count your clouds before they hatch
Skin a needle
Go with the whir
Lick your horses
Crying over spilled mothers
Skin a lick
Hold your mother
Don't lick your chickens before they hatch

Untitled

By Ryan Heran

happy as a blackberry
lick your horses
skin a lick
don't lick the chickens
jumping on the needle
cat got your mother
skin a blackberry
mother your horses

Don't Be a Bandwagoner

By Anna Mattioli

Go unlike the flow
If your friend jumps off a bridge, don't
Licking cold poles on a shivery day won't do you any good
Reach for the clouds
Stop and pick the blackberries
Do something only you can do
Let out your voice.

Cheap

By Joseph Tartaglia

I like random words -
cliff, needle, voice, whir,
and blackberry are a few.
Others are cloud, mother,
and lick. They make me
happy as a clammy clam!
filler
filler
filler
filler

Praise Poems

Poets wrote poems modeled after the West African tradition of the praise poem, a form that asks the poet to name where they are from and to whom they belong while celebrating those qualities which make them unique

Who am I?
By Ashley Reed

Ashley Caelyn Reed
I was born in Danbury Hospital
In my free time, I ride horses
I am a horse because I am brave
I am as smart as a dolphin because I help people with math
I fear bees, and I will go near one someday
Lover of school
Ashley Caelyn Reed

Susannah S. Drap
By Susannah Drap

Susannah S. Drap
My name means Lily, I don't like my middle name, I am from
Sandy Hook CT.
I connect with horses, I work with them, ride them, and take
pictures of them.
I am a horse, sometimes nice, sometimes annoying.
I fear spiders and cruises. I overcame my fear of spiders by
my friend throwing them at me. I have yet to overcome my
fear of cruises because I refuse to get on a cruise ship.
Lover of horses, Helper of animals, Questioner of authority.
Susannah S. Drap

Chase Christopher Ewer Yeaton

By Chase Yeaton

Chase Christopher Ewer Yeaton
My name means hunter
I'm from Attleboro, Massachusetts
I love my hair
I am a leopard because I'm energetic and confident.
I am as smart as a dolphin
I am mortally terrified of spiders, and I try to overcome my fear
    of them by running for my life
Lover of food
Chase Christopher Ewer Yeaton

Joseph Karl Tartaglia

By Joseph Tartaglia

Joseph Karl Tartaglia
Means "he shall add" in Hebrew
From Italy and Sweden
Likes alone time
Is a rock for strength
Curious math mind
Feared dark, overcame by bravery
Lover of learning
Joseph Karl Tartaglia

Kaia Ryan Gioffre

By Kaia Gioffre

Kaia Ryan Gioffre
Kaia means the beautiful one in Hawaiian.
I am from Newtown Ct.
I have a pigmentation disorder.
I am a hurricane because you never know when I am coming.
I love to run.
I am very confident about my self.
I'm afraid of loosing my family.
Kaia Ryan Gioffre

About Me Poem

By Emilee Christopher

Emilee Noel Christopher
Adopted form China
All Chinese
I was a orphan
I am a horse cause I love to run
I can skateboard
Swimming in the ocean, I just do it.
Caring for others
Emilee Noel Christopher

Maura Daly Drabik

By Maura Daly Drabik

Maura Daly Drabik

Gaelic for Mary

Daughter of the Emerald Isle

Once high stepped with The Barrett Pipers and Dancers

Now like a wave, seeing years rush in and ebb out to sea

Known to have a song for every occasion

Fear heights, yet climbed the stairs of China's Great Wall

Born to Teach

Maura Daly Drabik

Kate Marie Farrington

By Kate Farrington

Kate Marie Farrington
The name Marie comes from my moms mom
I am from Bridgeport
I am shy but I don't show it that much
I would be the sun because I am Bright
I am sweet as a sweet apple
I fear bees but I learned to ignore them
Helper at everything
Kate Marie Farrington

Todd Michael Stentiford

By Todd Stentiford

Todd Michael Stentiford
A tod is a fox, Uncle Michael's Godson
Half English, then scrambled fractions European
I have been rescued by strangers (angels) more than once
I am water, spreading out, exploring, freezing, thawing, rushing, dripping
I am a comfortable corner painted brightly, sheltering thinkers, dreamers, eye-openers
Audiences frighten me, so I play the fool, you smile and I am at ease
Nostalgic Musical Dad
Todd Michael Stentiford

What I'm made of

By Bridget Gogliettino

Bridget Hope Gogliettino
My name means strength
I am Irish
I have gold in my eyes
I am a river because I go with the flow, I try not to worry
I am as free as a bird, I give people hope and cheer them up when they are low
I fear that I will make mistakes but I learned that no one cares if I do
Funny, Cheerful, Hopeful
Bridget Hope Gogliettino

Praise Poem

By Luke Sordi

Luke Nicholas Sordi
My last name means a group of deaf people
Irish on the outside, Italian on the inside
I am open to new opinions and ideas
I am life for my interest of death
I am creative which makes for strange talk at the lunch table
I was scared of spiders but I overcame my fear by accepting nature
I am an evil genius master-mind
Luke Nicholas Sordi

Anna Elizabeth Romano

By Anna Romano

Anna Elizabeth Romano
My grandmother's middle name
Italy is where I'm from
I am humorous in my own way
I am a tiger because I am fierce
I sing for people to listen
My flashlight shines to prevent my fear
Lover of dance
Anna Elizabeth Romano

Self reflect
By Thomas Gies

Thomas James Gies
My first name is my granddad's and my middle name is my grandpa's
I am from Newtown, CT
I swim
I am a eagle because I want to see the world
I am outgoing. This makes people happy
I am scared of bees and I conquer that by running away like Usian Bolt
Lover of animals
Thomas James Gies

Ryan Charles Heran
By Ryan Heran

Ryan Charles Heran
my name means kingly
newtown, connecticut
as smart as a wizard
i fear jelly fish
lover of pizza
eater of food
lover of ball
Ryan Charles Heran

Me

By Michael Patrick Elston

Michael Patrick Elston
The commanding Ark Angel
The patron saint of Ireland
I'm German, Irish, English, and many more
I'm aggressive like my dad
I'm like a wolf strong and protective
I'm good at whistling which can hurt people's ears
I was afraid of wasps well I still am
I am loyal, a questioner of answers and dangerous ally
I am Michael Patrick Elston

ADEM SELMANI

By Adem Selmani

ADEM SELMANI
my name means first man on earth
i am from albania
I am muslim
i would be a volcano cause i erupt at home
i fear i will let my team down i overcame it by not letting them down
lover of soccer
eater of chocolate
ADEM SELMANI

Hannah Sophia Sepp
By Hannah Sepp

Hannah Sophia Sepp
After Johannah O'shey
My Heritage is from all over the world but I am true to Newtown CT
I am a little Dyslexic
Being shy, fears ,loving and more I am like a fox
as most know I am strong willed and never give up
I am afraid of people
But I am The voice of many animals
Hannah Sophia Sepp or technically Johannah Sophia Akecheta Sepp

Michael Haddick
By Michael Haddick

Michael Haddick
I am from Newtown, Connecticut
My true passion is skateboarding
I am an eagle because I am quick and high flying
I am a snake because I can be sneaky
I had a fear of heights but I overcame it on a roller coaster
Lover of the outdoors
Michael Haddick

Collaborative Around the Table Poems

Poets wrote collaboratively around the workshop table, responding only to the line directly above the one the poet was composing. This exercise is inspired by Richard Hugo's idea that "it is impossible to write meaningless sequences," and "in a sense the next thing always belongs." All poems began with a phrase, either "from here, I . . ." or "no one is here, and . . . ," and then followed a set of identical sentence-driven prompts. Each poet wrote one line and then passed the poem to the right. Since these poems were written collaboratively, no poet's name appears as author. Also included is a metaphor portrait of the cluster written collaboratively and including a line by every class member.

Pie

From here, I watched the sun set.
The red and orange ball sinking through the blue ocean.
The sky turns dark, and one by one twinkling stars show themselves.
This paper fills me with anguish as I tell you my tale,
my tale of living heaven on Earth.
The sky was blue, with clouds drifting in it, I liked it.
The tennis whizzed through the air like a speedy bullet.
It burns through the air like pepper on my tongue.
The sky turns black, and my heart sings.
My heart sings for my kite that I fly in the wind.
I swam in the ocean with my friends.
I wish I could dunk.

Confusion

From here, I lollipops.
My favorite color is blue.
The night sky is as bright as the sun.
I wrote yellow written with a neon marker.
I like orange dots.
Comma, comma, three commas.
As many commas as the scouter's power level, OVER 9,000.
Air is wonderful, without it, we wouldn't be living.
I feel like yellow written with a neon marker, so bright
and happy on this wonderful day.
I have a folder with orange dots in it.
Look at the lollipop trees.
I wish my power level was OVER 9,000!!!

Making Sense

From here, I will always make sense.
Blue is blue and green is green and that is how it always should be.
The sky is happy, so why is it blue.
Animals do not wear clothes,
though lions retain the right to a mane.
There is a comma, and another comma, and another.
Like is a word as as is a word.
Not like each other but both the same like dogs from the same pack.
Blue and white.
This paper is on a desk, being written on.
Green is new and life-filled and envied by all, especially its cousin, Brown.
I want a wish.

Randomnis

No one is here, and now I am alone.
My favorite color is turquoise.
The only thing that is left with me is the sky.
I like book.
It is Friday, May 22, 2015.
The moment you feel it, it's coming, why now?
I am awesome, as a narwhal is.
There are a lot of people here.
I saw a cloud shaped as a bird in the sky.
I go on the computer.
My shirt is turquoise.
I wish I had goat.

Untitled

From here, I ran a mile.
All I can see is purple.
There is an airplane in the sky.
There are many books in the library.
One of my favorite books is *Maze Runner*.
I am awesome, I rock too, also, I am cool.
My shirt is as blue as the sky.
I drank from my water bottle.
Bird flew in sky.
I am holding my notebook.
The mile kills my legs.
I wish everybody would stop saying my name.

Random

No one is here, and no one can hear us.
And the sky is blue as blueberries.
The sky is a light shade of orange.
The notebook lies across the big tan desk.
Do not hit my brother.
Please give me the butter, bread and cheese, please.
You're as red as a tomato.
The paper was white as snow before I wrote my essay.
The textbook was on a tan desk.
The computer was glitching every other second.
Perhaps you didn't notice that we are blueberries.
I wish I could stay above the clouds.

Nothing

From here, I stay alone doing nothing.
Gazing at the dark wall, wishing to see the blue sky.
The sky always fills me with bliss until I begin to grow curious,
letting my mind wander.
I sit at my table thinking about a theory of everything.
I love holidays!
I like playing basketball, tennis, etc.
A dragonfly darts through the air, as fast as a jet.
It could be a cat poster, so serene.
The sky always fills me with bliss, giving me a theory of everything.
I need paper to write on!
I ate my bagel, doing nothing else.
I wish my house was made of gold.

The Pineapple Revolution

No one is here, and the pineapple revolution is about to
overthrow the White House!
From now on it'll be known as the yellow house.
As bright as the sky , as dark as the sea—
Gowy, sticky, wet. Squish it, form it, splash it. Ooblick!
This sentence is exactly eight words (not).
Although that was funny, I'm now focused on punctuation,
as you should be.
The pineapple revolution was as large as an entire farm's worth,
and got bigger every day.
Pineapples are not water, but water is the only water there is.
Squish it, form it, splash it, watery water!
Lollipops you can get anywhere, the store, the doctor, your sister.
The yellow submarine is yellow.
Your wish is my hope is her prayer is their longing
can be our reality.

We Are

A Cluster Metaphor Portrait by the Drabifordians

We are a generation of new thinkers.
We are daisies in a field of roses.
We are rainbows, colorful but mysterious.
We are all special in our own way.
We are far from ordinary.
We are able to make school fun.
We are strong in every way.
We are a bright light bulb, bright as any other.
We are shadows following our leader.
We are birds spreading their wings for the first time.
We are one raindrop in a storm.
We are eagles in the sky.
We are leprechauns trying to get to the other side
of the rainbow.
We are one unique team.
We are lucky like a four leaf clover.
We are the knowledge of the future.
We are the sun shining bright.
We are the burning flames in a fire.
We are not soup cans, labeled items put on shelves.
We are Drabifordians, equal as ourselves.
We are the rainbow that puts color in your day.
We are pebbles on a mountain.
We are the sun that brightens everybody's day.
We are blank slates. We are open minds.
We are notebooks waiting to be written in.
We are Legos, interlocking to create the perfect creation.
We are the sun rising.
We are the fish in the river of life.
We are flowers waiting to bloom.
We are the good inside a day!
We are unique in our own way!
We are energetic.
We are silly like a careless kid.

We are bright like the sun.
We are all different in our own special way!
We are a footprint left in the sand.
We are one violin in an orchestra.
We are always looking forward to the best of times.
We are the sparks of a fire.
We are the darkness seeping up from below.
We are the stars shining in the midnight sky.
We are all wonderful stories waiting to be read.
We are optimistic.
We are like stars, invisible to most, but burning brightest
before we fade.
We are time.
We are the brightest stars up in the midnight sky.
We are powerful in the way we can change our world.
We are bold, like the wolf against the full moon.
We ain't chickens.
We are unique like a regular human.
We are the Drabifordians.

Contributors

Elijah Baraw: I am imaginative, curious, and strive to learn. I like poetry because it allows me to express my true self.

Joseph Bonsignore is an avid gamer who enjoys to just sit back and relax. He wrote about the Chocolate Thunder because Outback is his favorite restaurant.

Hi, I am **Anne Marie Carlson**. I am eleven and am in Mr. Stentiford's class. I have a certain love for poetry and I feel that I have a good sense for it. On behalf of myself and the cluster, I really would like to thank Mrs. Doherty for her hard work and I wanted to let her now that we all really appreciated it, Thanks Again!

Sophia Child: Hi! My name is Sophia and I am 12 years old. I love playing soccer and giving my cat belly-rubs.

My name is **Emilee Christopher** and I love to ride horses.

Maura Drabik: I am one half of the duo that has the lucky fortune of teaching forty- nine beautiful sixth grade Drabifordians.

CJ Demers: I am 12 years old and I have 2 brothers and 1 sister. I love to play baseball, basketball, and football. I enjoy winning and having fun with friends and my family.

Willem Doherty loves being a Drabifordian so much that he made a custom T-shirt line for his class and helped create a class seal. In his spare time he solves the Rubiks cube.

I'm **Julia Dolan**, and I am 11 years old. I love playing basketball, and hanging out with my bird, Mango.

My name is **Susannah Drap**, I am 11 years old.

Michael Patrick Elston: Hi, I'm Michael Elston. I play basketball and soccer.

Paige Farley, Kate Farrington, and **Nicholas Fischer** are Drabifordians.

Annie Fowler: I am Annie Fowler and I dance and play hockey. I have two older brothers and a twin sister.

Hi! I'm **Chelsea Fowler** and I am a student at RIS. I enjoy doing ballet and playing guitar and cello, and gardening. I live with my mom, dad, 2 brothers, twin sister, and my dog Dahlia.

Thomas Gies: About me: I am 11 years old. I love sports. I go to Reed Intermediate School.

Kaia Gioffre: My name is Kaia. My. Big dream is to go to UCSD and graduate as a valedictorian and become a teacher or a physical therapist. And become a mother later in life.

Bridget Gogliettino: I'm 12 years old. I like to swim and I like reading.

Joanie Gogliettino: I'm fascinating. You should get to know my writing.

Michael Haddick: I'm 12 years old. I like poetry because I get to write about my favorite sports, basketball and Lacrosse.

Ryan Heran: At the time of publishing I was 12 years old. I like basketball and baseball.

Collin Hoffman is 12 years old and has two brothers. He plays lacrosse, soccer, and basketball.

Trevor Jacozzi: I'm eleven years old and I play baseball, football, and basketball. I enjoy sports and being competitive.

Rushil Jerfy At the time of publishing I was 12 years old. My favorite sports are tennis and basketball, oh and I kinda' have a guilty love for Pop-Tarts

Clayton Kunzweiler: I am 11 years old and I enjoy poetry because it allows me to break all the rules of writing I have ever learned.

My name is **Jennifer Lorenz**. I love doing anything with a pencil—writing or drawing, but I don't like typing. I also enjoy reading, tennis, and basketball. One more thing I love is music. I play the piano and cello and love them both.

Allie Luby: I am in a family of five. I love to play softball, golf, and skiing.

Shaine Luzietti: I am twelve years old. I enjoy playing sports.

Zack Majeski: About my two poems: I found a similar poem in a book, and while it isn't a normal false apology, it rhymes, and makes it even funnier. I couldn't come up with any metaphors for this poem until I found different objects that symbolized me in different ways, and it all came together to form my metaphor portrait.

Anna Mattioli is a hard-working, fun, creative 6th grader. She attends Reed Intermediate School in Newtown, CT. Anna's passion for writing and love of school fuel her creativity. She loves all types of animals(dogs especially) and is thrilled to be published in a book. :)

Douglas McIntyre: Hey, I'm Douglas I love the army also I love to build I'm 12 years old I play football, Wrestling, basketball flag, football and base ball and I am unique.

Juliana Miraldi: I enjoy writing novels because they let me get my feelings out on paper.

Lauren Nalajala: I am 11 years old and I love to read.

Abby Poseno: I am 12 years old and I love lacrosse. I have two cats and 2 hamsters. The cat's names are Brady and Sox. The hamsters are kiwi and pumpkin. I enjoy 3D drawing and when I grow up I either want to be an architect of a veterinarian (vet).

Paige Psichopaidas: Hi my name is Paige I am 12 years old and my big dream is to become a doctor just like my sister. She inspires me so much. I hope I can be just like my sister Erica!

Hi, my name is **Ashley Reed**. I am 11 years old. In my free time I like to ride horses, read, and draw. I really enjoy school. My favorite subject is math. I play the violin and I really love it. I also like to sing.

Brynn Reilly: I decided to write about being unique because it is important to be yourself.

Jenna Reilly: I am eleven years old. I enjoy playing basketball and softball.

Anna Romano: I enjoy dancing.

Noelle Salley: I love to read!

Adem Selmani: I am eleven years old and I enjoy soccer.

Hannah Sepp: I love animals and have many pets.

Patrick Sonne: I am awesome.

My name is **Luke Sordi** and I'm in sixth grade. I am twelve years old, have a younger brother, and a yellow lab. I have done poetry in school as a unit twice before this unit so it was pretty new, but I definitely had fun doing it.

Todd Stentiford: I am the 'iford of Drabiford. It has been an honor to know and teach this beautiful group of learners.

Jack Street is athletic, caring, happy, smart, fun.

John Sullivan: I am eleven years old and I love sports.

Joseph Tartaglia is a Junior Black Belt, golfer, and swimmer. He likes to play basketball, build with LEGO bricks, and play video games. He also likes having time with his family. He doesn't know for sure what he wants to be, but he might be a scientist, doctor, mathematician, or programmer.

Julian Totir: I like sports, science and origami.

Chase Yeaton: I love soccer and free running!

Drabifordian Index of Poets

CPSIA information can be obtained at www.ICGtesting.com
Printed in the USA
BVOW03s0859080615

403444BV00003B/3/P

9 780990 462965